NAUGHTY NIPPER

WRITTEN BY

C.J. SUGIE

ILLUSTRATED BY

BRUCE CLARK

Archway Publishing books may be ordered through booksellers or by contacting:

Archway Publishing
1663 Liberty Drive
Bloomington, IN 47403
www.archwaypublishing.com
1 (888) 242-5904

Because of the dynamic nature of the Internet, any web addresses or links contained in this book may have changed since publication and may no longer be valid. The views expressed in this work are solely those of the author and do not necessarily reflect the views of the publisher, and the publisher hereby disclaims any responsibility for them.

Any people depicted in stock imagery provided by Thinkstock are models, and such images are being used for illustrative purposes only.
Certain stock imagery © Thinkstock.

ISBN: 978-1-4808-2467-6 (sc)
ISBN: 978-1-4808-2468-3 (e)

Print information available on the last page.

Archway Publishing rev. date: 1/5/2016

DADDY BOUGHT US A PONY ONE NIGHT, WHO NIPPED HIM IN THE BEHIND.

DADDY NAMED OUR PONY THAT NIGHT AND NIPPER WOULD BE HIS NAME.

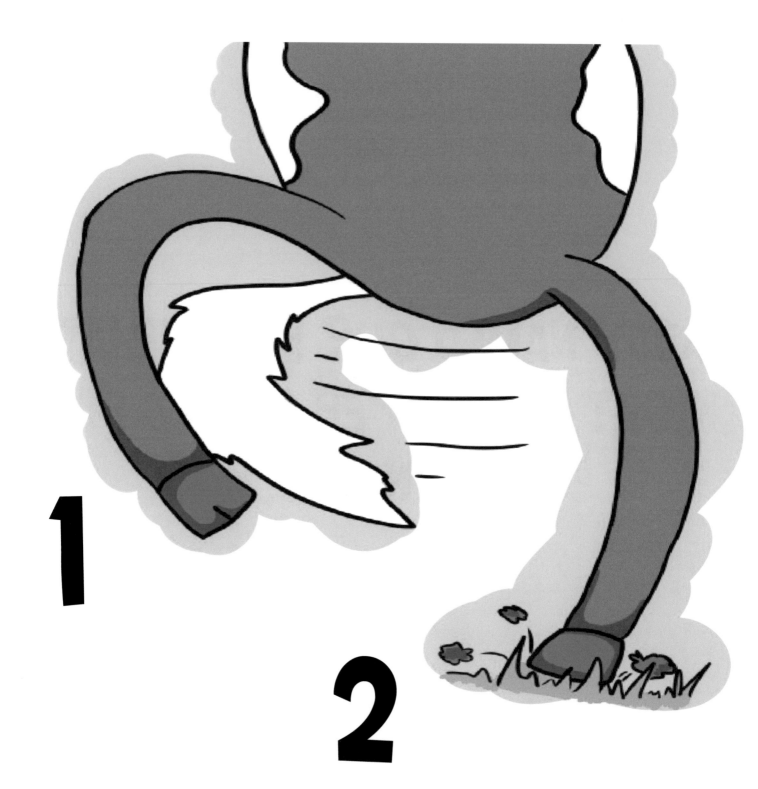

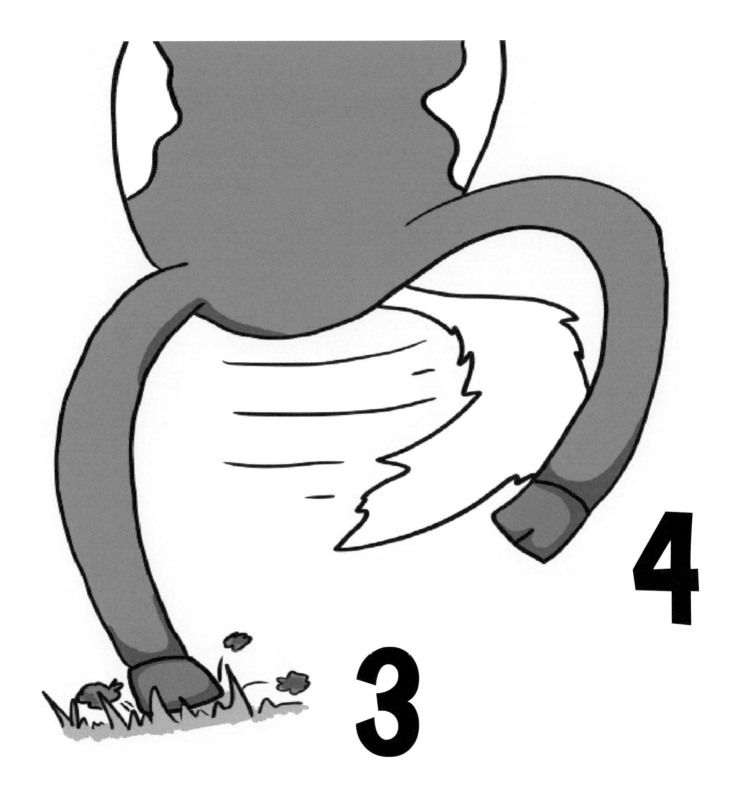

NAUGHTY NIPPER, MY
NAUGHTY, NAUGHTY, NIPPER.

NAUGHTY NIPPER, MY
NAUGHTY, NAUGHTY, NIPPER.

NEXT DAY, SISTER SUSIE, DECIDES TO RIDE OUR NEW PONY.

RUNNING DOWN THE FIELD WITH SISTER SUSIE, SCREAMING, "HELP ME!!"

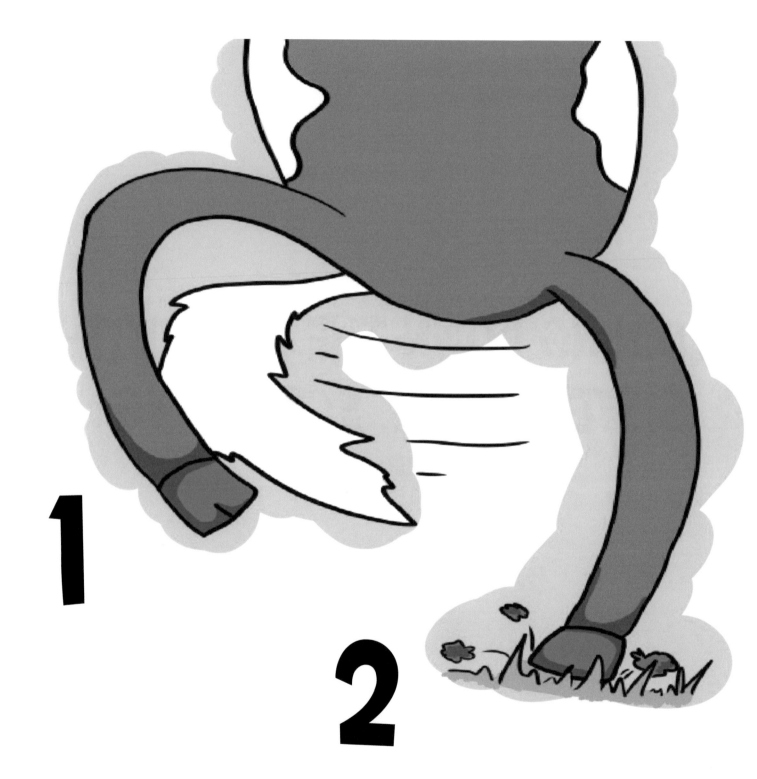

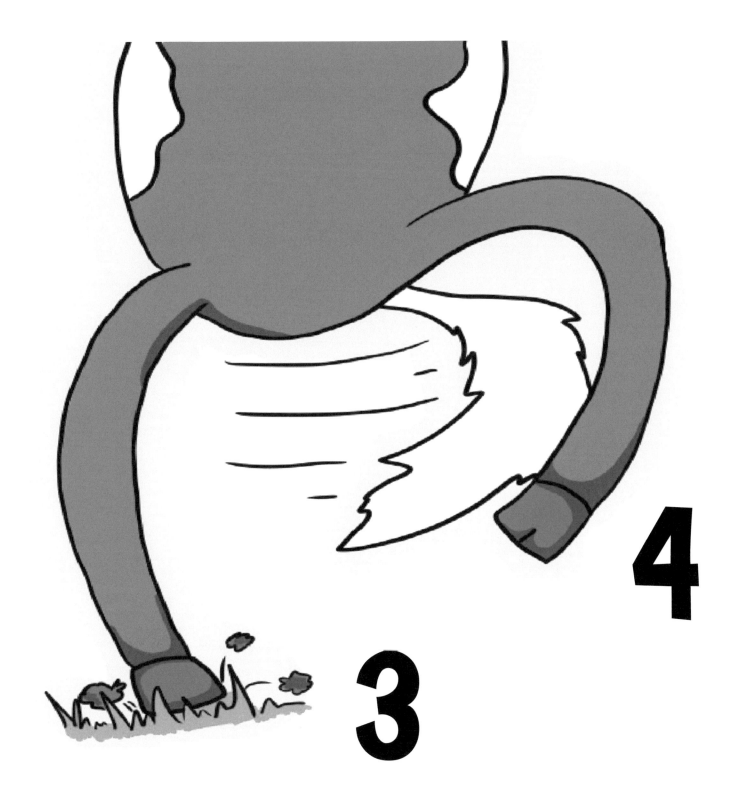

NAUGHTY NIPPER, MY NAUGHTY, NAUGHTY, NIPPER.

NAUGHTY NIPPER, MY
NAUGHTY, NAUGHTY, NIPPER.

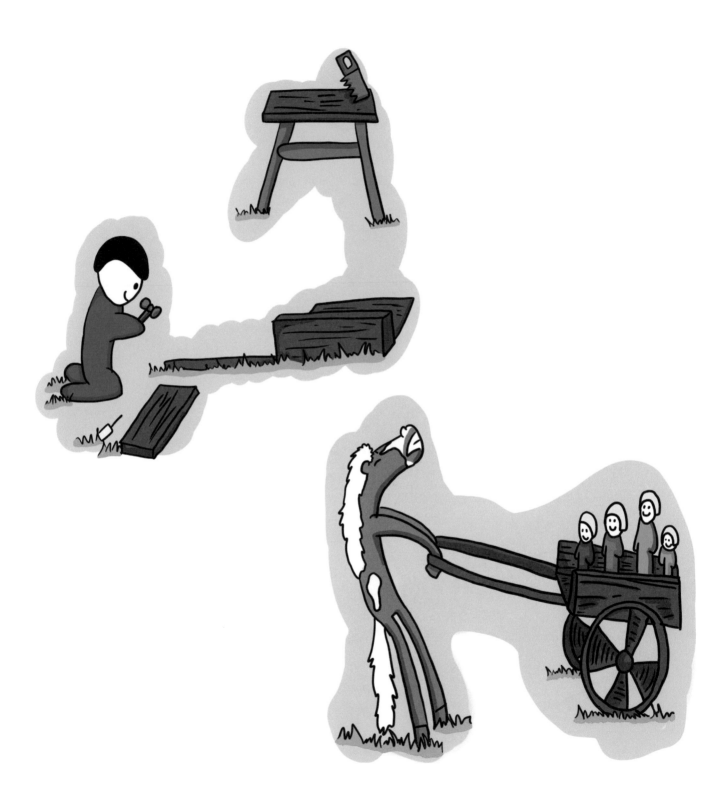

DADDY BUILT US SOME PONY CARTS AND NIPPER TOOK US FOR THE RIDES.

NIPPER GOT SPOOKED ONE CRAZY DAY AND TOOK US THROUGH THE NEIGHBOR'S YARD.

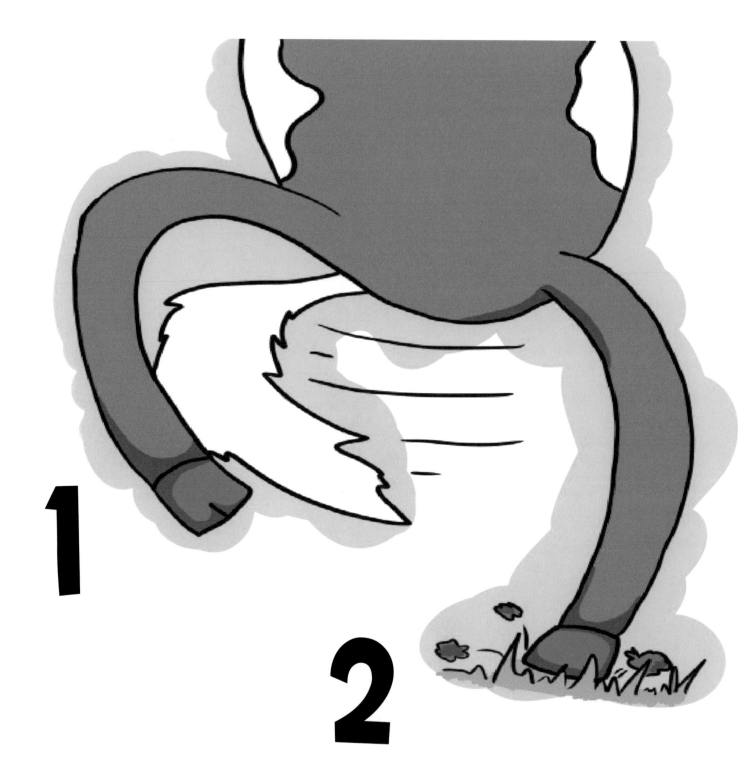

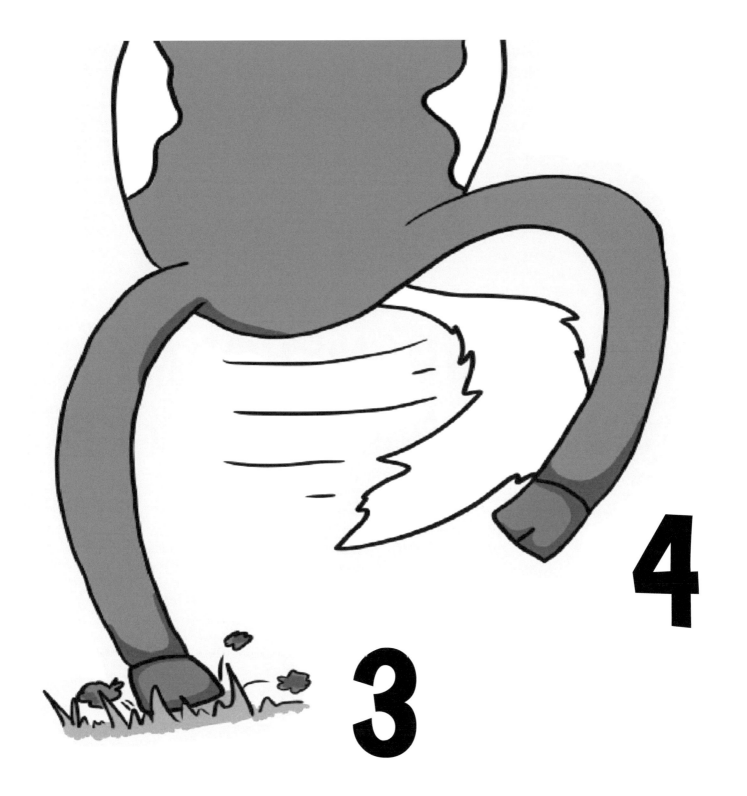

NAUGHTY NIPPER, MY NAUGHTY, NAUGHTY, NIPPER.

NAUGHTY NIPPER, MY
NAUGHTY, NAUGHTY, NIPPER.

NIPPER TOOK US FISHING ONE DAY. WE CROSSED A METAL BRIDGE.

NIPPER'S FOOT WENT THROUGH A HOLE AND WE WENT FLYING!

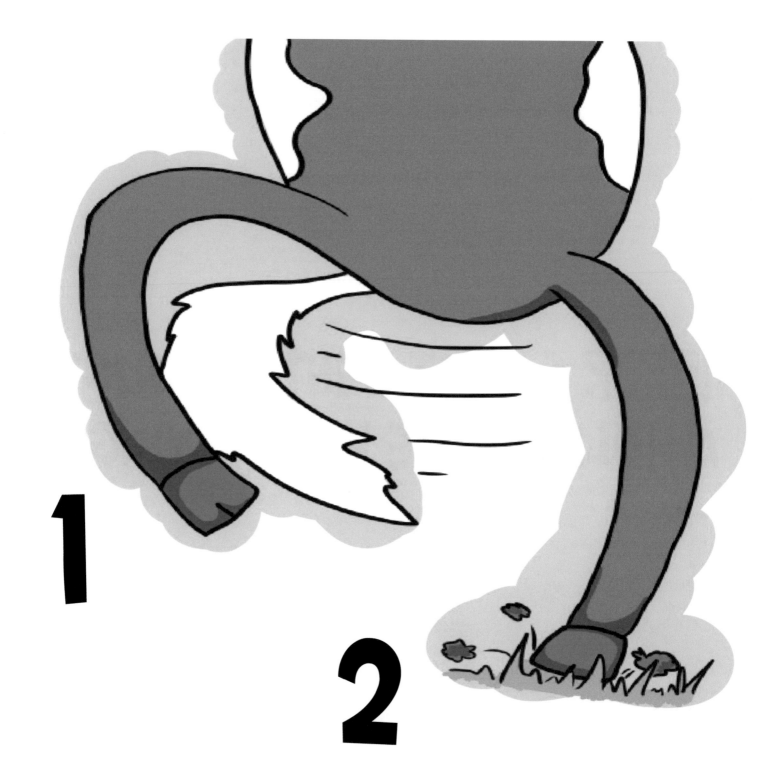

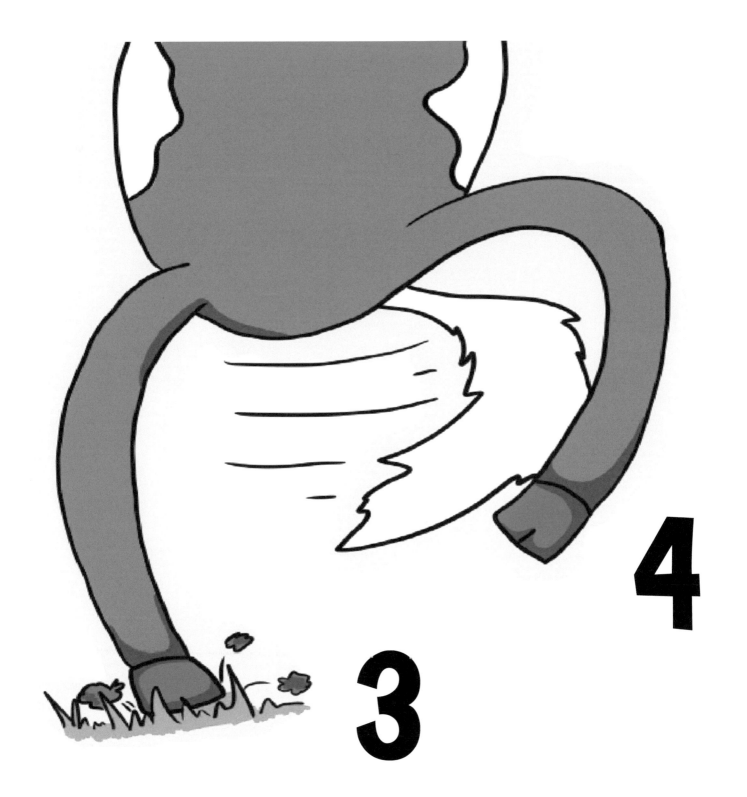

NAUGHTY NIPPER, MY
NAUGHTY, NAUGHTY, NIPPER.

NAUGHTY NIPPER, MY NAUGHTY, NAUGHTY, NIPPER.

WHEN HE WAS OLD, HE WENT TO A FARM, TO GRAZE THE PASTURES.

I'LL NEVER FORGET NAUGHTY NIPPER AND ALL OF OUR ADVENTURES.

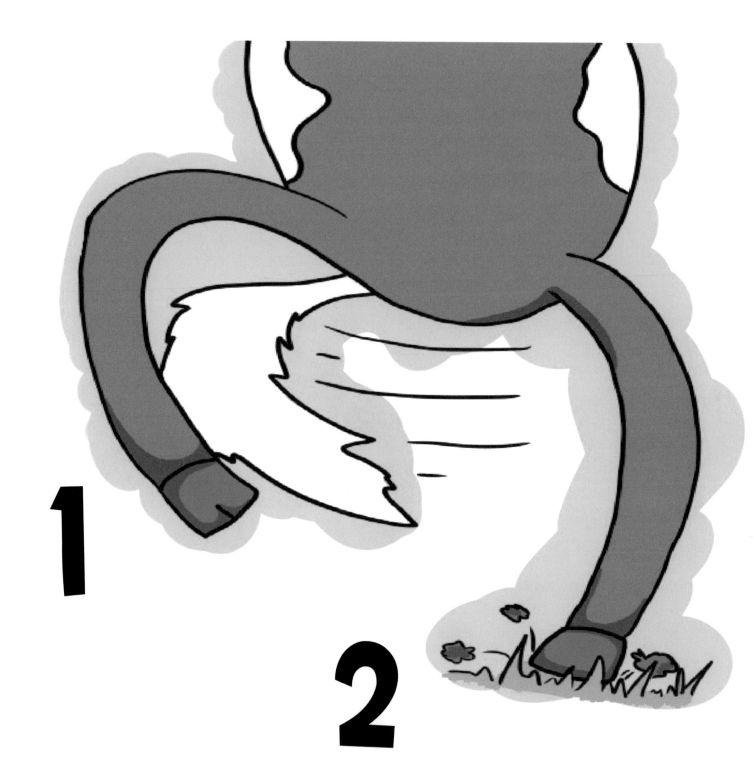

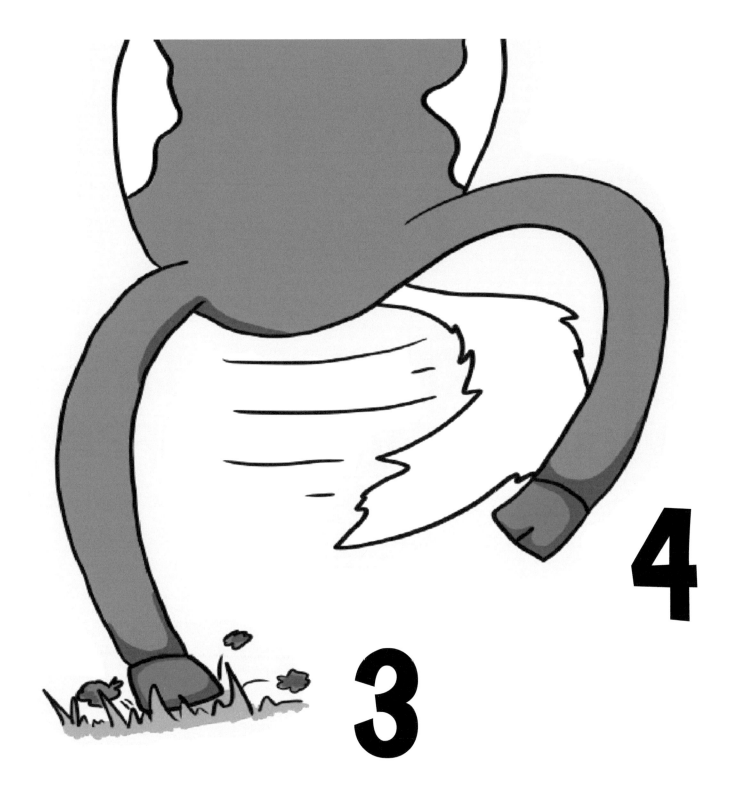

NAUGHTY NIPPER, MY
NAUGHTY, NAUGHTY, NIPPER.

NAUGHTY NIPPER, MY
NAUGHTY, NAUGHTY, NIPPER.

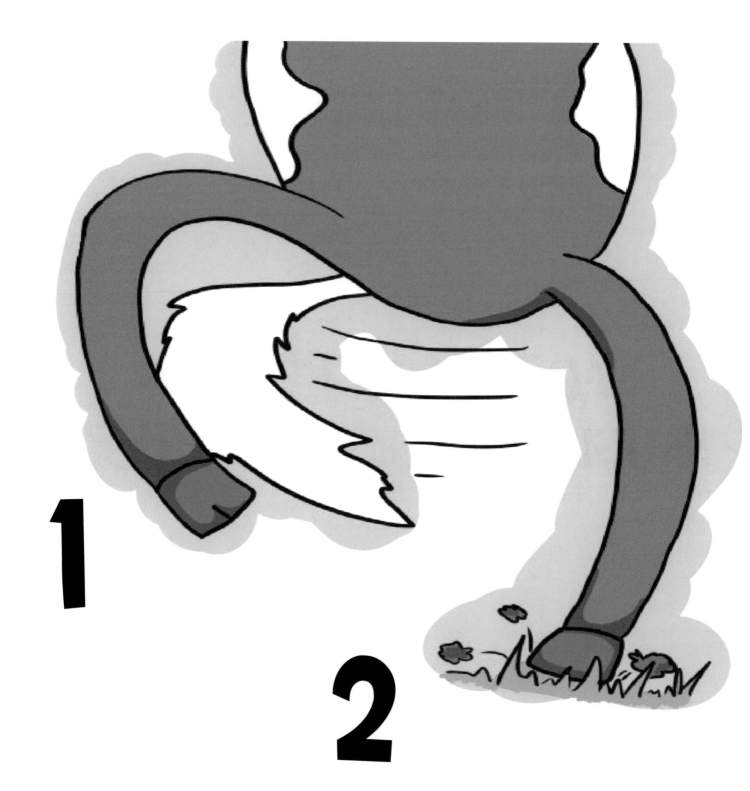

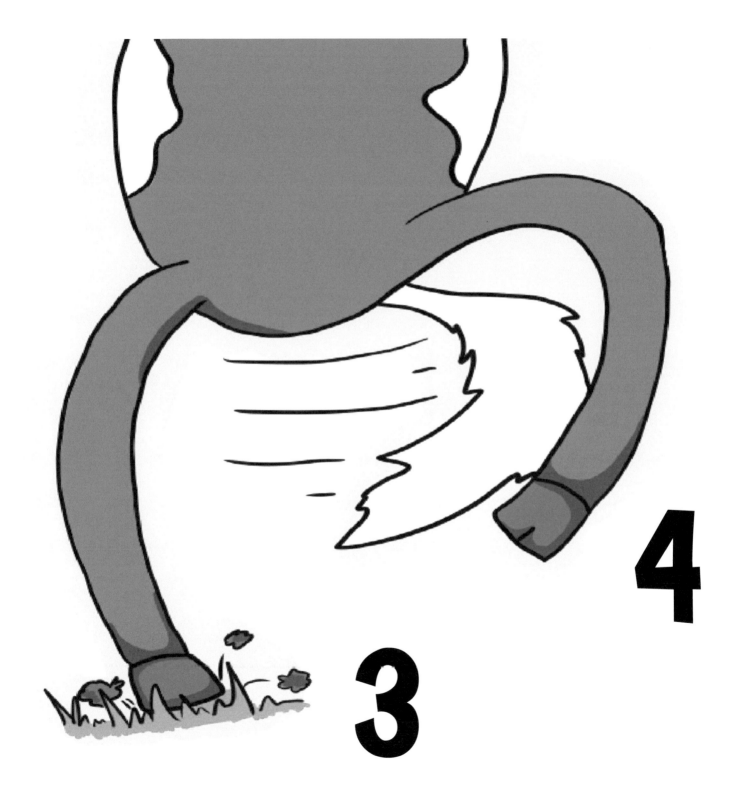

MISS MY NAUGHTY NIPPER!

Printed in the United States
By Bookmasters